COPYRIGHT NOTICE

Image source:

❖ Template images with permission from Template.Net

❖ Other images used under license from 123rf.com

❖ Mock-ups by smartmockups.com

INTRODUCTION

The interior design business is a complex and multifaceted one, and it goes way beyond the creative and imaginative. There is indeed an aspect of the business that is exciting, colourful, and perhaps showy, but it is not all as rosy as it appears. The artistic side of interior design may be fun, but it is the business aspect of the profession that brings in most of the revenue. To run a successful interior design business no matter what its size may be, a designer must not only be inventive and artsy, he/she must also be resourceful and business-oriented.

There is no doubt that the commercial side of interior design is not as exciting as the artistic side. It involves branding, planning, organising, allocating duties, creating employment, managing projects, and working out time schedules. An interior designer must be adept in records documentation, materials procurement, site supervision, and market analysis. This is the complex part of interior design.

Running a multi-dimensional business like interior design requires special business tools. From special ink pens and interior design workbooks to niche-specific templates and software applications, these tools are needed to implement tasks successfully and profitably. So, whether you work solo, as a freelancer, just starting out, or a veteran in the industry, a business is only successful if it is backed up with the right working tools.

In this handbook, you will find the important tools you need to run your business in an organised and professional way. If you desire a good working relationship with stakeholders, clients, customers, consultants, and working teams, these tools are essential. If you want your brand to grow profitably you need more than your imaginative talents. Without the right business tools, there will be blunders, oversights, undue pressure, loss of revenue, or worse still, litigations.

With the right collection of interior design-specific tools, you will effortlessly plan, organize, and implement near-seamless projects that will produce satisfied customers.

IMPORTANT BUSINESS TOOLS

Veteran interior designers, beginners, and students of interior design require basic tools to work with, but these are the most important ones. The must-haves.

While the requirements of veteran designers may differ from what students may need, there are still some basic tools that both the experts and novices must have in their arsenal of 'implements'. The good news is that these tools of the trade are simple and few.

Some of the most important business documents and implements you may need as a professional in the field are:

1. Interior design workbooks
2. Organisational templates
3. CAD software programs
4. Wet and dry media
5. Interior design Apps
6. Measuring tape
7. Colour wheel and charts
8. Camera
9. Samples and swatches - paint, wallpaper, fabric, etc...
10. Design publications
11. Portfolio

1. Interior Design Workbooks

To work professionally, interior designers require specific workbooks to help them both create beautiful design concepts and run their businesses optimally. These workbooks are created to keep details like client data, task logs, site measurements, contractor and sub-contractor details, vendor database, appointments, client questionnaires, and project management.

They also include workbooks needed to develop design concepts, sketch and draw ideas, draw perspective views, create look-books, logbooks, and much more.

EXAMPLES OF INTERIOR DESIGNWORKBOOKS

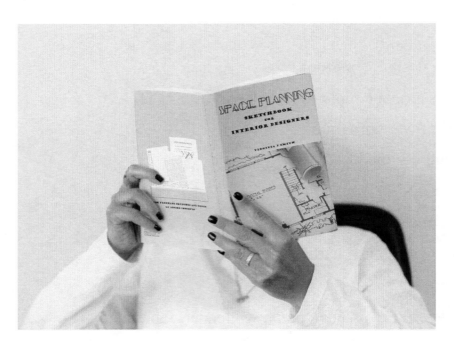

Space Planning Sketchbook for Interior Designers

https://www.amazon.com/dp/B08KH3R53Q

Measure, Sketch, and Dimension Notebook for Interior Designers

https://www.amazon.com/dp/B08F6CGC5M

Interior Design Project Management Logbook Journal

https://www.amazon.com/dp/B091WJ9YWN

Space Planning Sketchbook for Interior Design Students

https://www.amazon.com/dp/B0931X1P1D

Interior Design Project Manager – Challenges, Solutions, and Golden Rules

https://www.amazon.com/dp/B086PMZYV8

2. Organisational Templates

If you run an interior design firm, or if you work as a freelance designer or decorator, various organisational templates will be valuable for your business. They are ready-made and editable templates created to save you hours of tedious work. Using them will help you avoid situations where you may find yourself knee-deep in creating countless Microsoft Word and Excel spreadsheet documents. They include templates that will assist entrepreneurs in preparing quotations, contract proposals, contract agreements, work schedules, consultancy forms, client questionnaires, project schedules, task planners, and even letterheads and complimentary business cards.

EXAMPLES OF BUSINESS TEMPLATES

a) Interior Design Quotation Template

As the interior designer or representative of the firm, you must communicate the project's pricing in a very professional manner. But crafting a detailed quotation that covers every facet of a project can be a challenge for many interior designers. There are so many aspects of the job that can be easily overlooked, and this is not only bad for business, it can affect the company's profits adversely. A loose-ended mediocre quotation, will 'kill' any project even before it commences.

To avoid this, a professionally crafted quotation is important. It must communicate all prices and fees, including hidden costs, miscellanies outlay, and the necessary taxes. If you are in doubt about creating the perfect quotation, you can always use a task-specific template tool. And because they are editable and revisable, you can always modify them to suit the requirements of your interior design business.

Interior design quotation template

https://www.template.net/pro/10385/interior-design-quotation?ref=virginiasmith

b) Interior design contract agreement

This template is one of the most important interior design documents to have. If you are a freelance designer, a beginner, or one that has an established business, a signed agreement between you and the client is crucial for business. Terms and conditions must be laid out clearly and relevant clauses added to the formal document that will serve as a legally binding contract. This document will cover both parties against disagreements, acrimony, or in extreme cases, litigation. With a professionally generated template created by legal industry experts, you can create a customised contract agreement in less than a quarter of an hour.

Interior design contract agreement template

https://www.template.net/pro/10752/interior-designer-contract?ref=virginiasmith

c) Interior design proposal template

One of the most tiresome things about interior design consultation is drafting a business proposal. It is not always easy to get it super-professional. To combat this inadequacy at creating one, a great tool to have is an interior design proposal template specially crafted for interior designers by a professional interior designer.

This editable template is a must-have business tool. It will not only save you the money you will need to pay a professional to draft one, but it will also save you the time it will take to craft a detailed one if you prefer to do it yourself.

Interior design proposal template

https://www.template.net/pro/9041/interior-design-proposal?ref=virginiasmith

d) Interior design portfolio template

If you wish to create an interior design portfolio without the hassle of trying to figure out the best layout possible, this template tool is what you need. If you are a beginner designer, a student of interior design, or a veteran who wants something impressive to showcase proficiency and attract prospects, then this business template is it. Building an interior design portfolio goes beyond eye-catching mood boards with neatly arranged sketches, swatches, and images. To create a professionally documented portfolio that speaks volumes, this ready-made easy-to-modify portfolio-creation template specifically made for interior designers is designed with an impressive front and back cover. With sixteen landscape orientation pages, it is easy to customize text, images, and colours to suit your company's requirements.

Interior design portfolio template

https://www.template.net/pro/32306/interior-design-portfolio?ref=virginiasmith

e) Interior design project schedule template

There are two different categories of interior design projects; residential and commercial. However, no matter its size or the task involved, every designer must have a project scheduling tool that communicates well to all stakeholders. It must specify what tasks need to be done. It must mention when they need to be done and how they are going to be implemented. It must document which resources will be delegated, to whom, and when. It must also indicate who is mandated to do what, and the timeframe in which all works will be completed.

For any project to be successfully implemented, without a detailed and well-documented project schedule, the entire project is bound for possible failure. To avoid working in a shoddy and plan-less manner, you can use a ready-made, editable, easy-to-customize, and printable project schedule template that is specially crafted for interior designers.

Interior design project schedule template

f) Interior designer letterhead template

An interior designer's letterhead must reflect the profession. While some may not agree with this, others know that without an impressive letterhead, you will be buried in the sea of prospects-seekers. An interior designer's company letterhead must symbolise the business both aesthetically and effectively. It must possess a pleasant style in the way that it incorporate details like name, logo, address, and contact specifics. It must also be uncomplicated but attractive enough to create an outstanding visual representation of the interior design profession.

Interior design letterhead template

https://www.template.net/pro/22228/interior-designer-letterhead?ref=virginiasmith

g) Home interior design business plan template

This is the perfect template needed to set up the documentation aspect of an interior design business. Trying to create a professional business setup document with all the required specifics is not only challenging, but it is also time-consuming, especially when you try to create one from scratch. This template is a tool that makes a start-up meaningful and impactful. It is content-ready, editable, printable, and downloadable.

Having a perfectly crafted and well-organised business plan is tantamount to planning smartly to make better business decisions. Panning smartly will ensure you are working professionally. This approach will make your interior design business grow professionally and exponentially, and subsequently, increase your company's profits.

Home Interior Design Business Plan Template

https://www.template.net/pro/19338/home-interior-design-business-plan?ref=virginiasmith

EXAMPLES OF DESIGN & CONSULTANCY TEMPLATES

Interior design resume template

Your resume is your selling point. It represents many of your attributes; from your educational background to your work history, skills description, and some other details that must leave a lasting impression on prospects. As an interior designer trying to 'sell' him/herself, you must regard your resume as a special tool that presents you to potential clients or employers. This is where the use of professionally crafted interior design resume templates come into play. They will inspire and help you create the perfect CV to showcase your expertise to those you wish to impress and who matter to your business.

Interior design consultancy brochure template

Interior design firms have brochures that help to promote the company and the services it provides. The brochure must be well-designed and engaging enough to win over prospective clients and other customers that require interior design or interior architecture services. All the services provided must be highlighted with emphasis on billing structures, customer services, team introduction, etc... The information included must be brief but straight to the point. Using this upfront approach has worked perfectly for many interior designers as it helps to improve the company's marketing approach and promotional strategy.

Interior design newspaper template

If you are a practising interior designer, a design student, an e-publisher or run an interior design agency, you can create newsprints for everything interior design and decoration related. With this template tool, you can craft a unique online or offline presence that features the latest design and furnishing trends. You can publish news about the industry's activities and emerging new players in the market. You can even present reports on related events within a locality.

An easy-to-modify interior design newspaper template like this will help designers create friendly newspapers and newsletters that can keep the interior design topic in the minds of homeowners, homemakers, and design enthusiasts in their business vicinity.

Interior design catalogue template

Do you want to create a physical brochure or an e-catalogue to showcase your top projects to promising prospects? Do you want a document that's a compilation of the best interior décor products that you wish to retail online or offline? Do you want something modern, eye-catching, and perhaps minimalistic as a catalogue for your interior design business? If your answer is yes, yes, and yes, then this interior design catalogue template is for your firm. The templates come with eye-catching front and back covers, four pages of original suggestive headings, and content that can be edited and printed accordingly. They also come with high-quality and royalty-free images and artworks in both landscape and portrait orientations.

Interior design LookBook template

A bit similar to a portfolio but not quite the same thing, an interior design LookBook serves the purpose of promoting and/or showcasing the different aspects of the profession. For instance, displaying a beautiful home's interior, a landscape layout, décor items and product lines, new trends, and styling ideas through a collection of images and photographs in a multi-paged eye-catching book. The purpose of creating an interior design LookBook is to convey all these messages in a striking visual display, and marketable light that's intended to inspire consumers and attract interested buyers.

Benefits of Using Interior Design Specific Templates

With so many versatile and useful online interior design business tools that you can utilise, you can save yourself the tedious task of creating everything from scratch. If you wish to get tasks done faster and professionally, it is best to use professionally created tools that are downloadable, easy to modify, and quick to share with clients and team members. With these business tools, you can:

- Create a company's brand identity and visibility.
- Build better, faster, and bigger business processes.
- Improve productivity through better communication with all stakeholders and the workforce.
- Plan and organize tasks better, clearer, and tidier.
- Discover smarter ways to work by saving time and money while streamlining your business with the necessary documents like customised receipts, invoices, order forms, reports, and sales statements.
- Create top-notch but affordable marketing strategies and presentations.
- Increase sales with eye-catching banners for advertisements.
- Create and customize legally compliant business documents to suit your type of interior design business.
- Strategize your next move through market analysis and customer research.
- Create company branding requirements like logos, business cards, catalogues, etc..., for distribution to potential interior design clients.
- Ensure that your design business stands out from the crowd.
- Possess effective business tools for creating and sharing promotional designs and services on social media platforms, websites, or blogs.

3. CAD Software Programs

CAD software programs are computer-aided design tools that every 21st-century designer is familiar with. There are very few interior designers without basic knowledge of CAD software and it is safe to say that every professional in this field has at least two different programs they use to create their design concepts.

If you are a residential or commercial building interior designer who desires to be ahead of the competition, you must be adept in the use of digital drawing tools. Because many of today's clients are tech-savvy, they have higher expectations and will assess you by your ability to impress them with visual presentations. Hand-drawn plans and elevations on drafting tables are now outmoded.

Some of the most popular and easy-to-use interior design software programs are:

- RoomSketcher
- Autodesk
- Chief Architect Home Designer
- SketchUp Pro
- SmartDraw.
- DreamPlan
- Home Designer Suite

While veterans of many years may not find it necessary to learn how to use software programs, if you are a student, a beginner, or someone who has been in practice for some years, you must learn how to use interior design software. It is good to know that having the skills to create computer-generated representations to help you take your clients on a virtual tour of their projects is an added plus.

4. Manual drawing and design tools

CAD software is not for every interior designer as some top professionals and veterans still prefer to create their design concepts with pen on paper. Pre-CAD, there was only one way to design and that was drawing on drafting boards with pencils, T-squares, protractors, templates, rulers, French curves, and special drafting paper. Each design layout of floor plans, elevations, sections, working drawings, and perspectives was painstakingly drawn by hand and sometimes it took weeks or months to complete design concepts. Some 'old-school' designers still miss this technique. They love the feel of drawing on drafting paper or in niche-specific sketchbooks using the old-reliable tools – pencils and pens. Other popular drawing mediums are felt tips, charcoal sticks, and surprisingly, crayons.

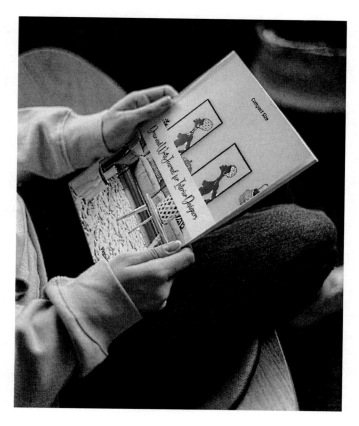

Compact Size Draw and Write Journal for Interior Designers: A Portable Sketchbook for Interior Design Illustrations and Notes

Designing with manual tools requires a knowledge of drafting which is taught extensively in the first year of design school. The technical drawing skills acquired in design school will go a long way in helping students understand how to draw to scale, work out perspectives and projection lines, and create interior design working drawings.

Even with today's cutting-edge technology, knowing how to draw relatively well is still necessary. So, although being proficient in the use of design software programs is essential, every professional will still need to make quick sketches now and then especially while consulting with a prospective client or while trying to clarify a point with the workforce.

5. Interior design apps

Most interior designers are familiar with, and have used at least one interior design app at one point in their career and being app-savvy is now a part of being a successful designer. Today, with some top interior design application, a designer can showcase everything that can be stored in a heavy portfolio case in something as light as a smartphone or similar device.

With designer apps, one can gather and store design ideas and inspirations, run day-to-day business activities, and plan and organise tasks. Apps can also be used for client-designer communications, and even assist in drawing simple design tasks. Examples of popular 4star+ interior design apps are:

- Home Design 3D
- Room Planner
- Live Home 3D
- Planner 5D
- Home Styler Interior Design
- Houzz Home Design & Renovation
- Ikea Place

Design apps are generally popular with beginner designers, students of interior design, and those who have a feel for home decoration apps.

6. Measuring tapes

This is perhaps the most important tool every designer needs and cannot do without. Interior designers depend on measuring tapes for every single form to be measured, including site measurements gauging, verifying, and calculating. Whether you are measuring a dining table, a kitchen nook, or a vaulted ceiling, this simple nondescript tool is a must-have.

While the traditional measuring tapes are meant for straight line/lengths, there are the cloth tapes which are best for measuring curvilinear and angled planes, and digital/electronic tapes that are the most accurate (to within 1/8" or 3mm), and the simplest to use. Laser tape measures have become a popular tool for savvy interior designers and those of us who like to stay current. The best laser tape measures, in no particular order, are:

- Dewalt Distance Laser
- Tacklife Classic
- Bosch Blaze Pro
- Bosch Bluetooth Enabled
- Morpilot Tape Laser

7. Colour wheel

Every interior designer should have a colour wheel chart. It is one business tool that sets an interior designer apart from the other professions in the building industry. You need a colour wheel to explain which colours will work with what, and how best to put them together so that they work harmoniously with each other.

Clients generally find colour wheels and the way they work fascinating, so, it is good to consider it an item that has the potential to highlight professionalism. It always appears like a scientific system that can generate pleasant colour schemes.

The colour wheel is necessary at almost every stage of the design process. It helps designers and artists arrive at both minor and major decisions for an entire concept. It can be consulted for everything, ranging from paint and wallpaper themes to choice of drapes, upholstery, rugs, soft furnishing, and other interior accents. It is a quick tool that can be used to find out what most appeals to a client's taste. And because colours are considered to be one of the most important elements that determine the feel and mood of interior spaces, getting the scheme right (or wrong) can make or break any interior design concept.

8. Digital Camera

Having a good digital camera is an added plus and as an interior designer, you should own one. A camera is a great tool that will help to create visual records of projects, job sites (think "before & after" shots), task stages, furnishing and accessories to show clients and customers. Some may feel that you don't need more than a phone's camera, an iPad, or any computer but just because you have one of these doesn't mean you will get the kind of professional images worthy of being added to your portfolio.

If you take subpar photos of your works, it will send the wrong message to your prospective clients/customers. They might just assume that your work will turn out crappy too and this is the sad truth. Investing in a camera doesn't have to cost that much. You don't have to pay thousands of dollars for an e-camera if you are on a tight budget. With as little as $250 (every interior designer can afford that), you can get this necessary business tool. All you need is to take high-enough quality pictures to add to your portfolio and showcase to prospects. Some efficient and affordable digital cameras any interior designer should find useful include:

- Canon EOS Rebel T6/EOS 1300D
- Olympus OM-D E-M10 Mark II
- Canon PowerShot SX530 HS Bundle
- Sony DSC-W810
- Fujifilm Instax Wide 300
- Kodak PixPro FZ43
- Canon PowerShot SX420 IS

9. Paint samples, wallpaper charts, and fabric swatches

Paint sample strips, wallpaper charts, fabric swatches, and catalogues with image samples of interior features like countertops, flooring, panelling, lighting fixtures, etc.., are a part of the important interior design tools every designer should possess.

Producers and manufacturers of home décor items and everything interior design related is more than happy to make provisions for professionals in the industry. The reasons for this are not farfetched; they need professionals in the industry to promote their product lines. These they do through their marketing strategies using books, charts, sample swatches, and all necessary elements a designer needs to sell her concept to prospective customers.

With these type of business tools, the interior designer can develop an interior space concept in just a couple of hours of consultation with a client who needs help selecting the right materials, their texture, and their feel to the touch. For instance, kitchen countertop materials, soft furnishings fabrics for throw cushions and window treatments, and, the texture and feel of wall coverings and upholstery fabrics.

This process is as important as the drawing and design development itself and is the time that your prospect can get a sense of how the finished product(s)/project will look and feel.

10. Portfolio

Nothing will promote you better as an interior designer than your previous works. And promising prospects need to see some of the tasks you have performed before being fully convinced about your expertise. A physical or digital portfolio is the business tool you need to convince them.

A sound portfolio that showcases your previous jobs and projects is vital for your integrity as a designer. Building a collection of design ideas, conceptual elements, plans, elevations, working drawings, renderings, forms and figures, sketches, and other works done over some time does wonders in building a designer's credibility and authority. A portfolio of high-quality photos with physical examples of relevant mood board items like fabric swatches, carpets samples, wall coverings, and other materials allows prospective clients to engage you more on a different level. Additionally, it will make them more trusting about your ability to deliver and also lend credibility to whatever service you offer.

Including copies of written reviews and testimonials from satisfied clients is an added plus and will add more impact than any other way you intend to market yourself.

Today, many designers add a digital portfolio (e-portfolio) to the mix, especially those who practice interior design online. An electronic version with carousels of images, videos of project executions, and filmed/recorded testimonials is a smart idea. With an e-portfolio, you can pitch your interior design business from wherever you to both local and international clients.

11. Magazines and publications

Magazines and publications serve more as reference materials than they do business tools, but it is good to have them in your arsenal as they help designers to keep abreast of market trends. Many interior designers find that they have amassed a great collection of design-related magazines. The older they have been in the business of interior design, the more magazine collections they have.

Asides from keeping designers abreast of new developments regularly, they also help to gain industry insights which can range from topics on the latest leanings of furniture forms and structure to the most talked-about design concepts of 2025.

Keeping yearly subscriptions for, at least, a couple of design publications is a great idea. You will also find them handy to show indecisive clients who have trouble expressing their design preferences. Knowing their inclinations at the early stages of consultation is a sure-fire way of getting speedy approvals.

12. Interior design coffee table-worthy books

When someone walks into an interior designer's home or office, they expect to see an array of interior design books. Coffee table books, reception lounge books, and waiting room books. They are mainly interior design related books about residential homes, commercial interiors, and landscape art. But all designers are different and their book collections are determined by their individual niches and interests. Many of these design-specific books are more picturesque than wordy, but then, as the popular adage goes, "a picture is worth a thousand words".

13. Client questionnaire books

An interior designer must never underestimate the power of a client questionnaire book. Presuming what the client wants can lead to disagreements. Verbal question and answer sessions are not enough to get the true picture of what they actually need from the designer. Working this way is not only unprofessional but is also bound to end up in dissatisfaction and in extreme cases, litigation.

Client questionnaire and organizer workbooks are important tools of the interior design business. It should be used to record client data, project information, design and decoration preferences, likes and dislikes, and other important information that will enable the designer to have a clear and detailed view of what a client really desires. Lifestyles, likes, loves, absolute dislikes, pet peeves, uncertainties, indecisions, etc..., all written down and documented in one questionnaire logbook.

Client Questionnaire Logbook for Interior Designers and Home Decorators: Documentation of Consultation between Customer and Designer

https://www.amazon.com/dp/B092H9V4YG

CONCLUSION

The success of an interior design business outfit is not only hinged on the designer's creative ability. Other things have to come into play. His or her working relationship with clients, other professionals in the industry, and the entire workforce is equally important. However, despite an all-encompassing set of skills, creativity, and wide technical knowledge, interior designers still require the right business tools to help run a successful and lucrative design company.

Having said all that, most of the business tools and implements required by interior designers are majorly affordable and, in many cases, can be acquired free of charge. Vendors, wholesalers, and manufacturers are always willing to give out samples like paint charts, fabric swatches, furniture catalogues, finishing samples, and even free downloads To work professionally, efficiently, and competently means to be professionally equipped with both digital and physical business tools that will help designers work faster, smarter, and in a more organised manner.

This is what "having an edge over your competitors" infers.

LINKS AND DISCLAIMER

AFFILIATE LINKS - This book contains affiliate links and the author will be compensated, at no extra cost to you if you make a purchase after clicking through a link.

DISCLAIMER - The content of this book is accurate and true to the best of the author's knowledge. It is not meant to substitute for formal and individualized advice. We have made sure to include trusted sites but bear no responsibility for any third-party products, services, or websites.

Made in United States
Cleveland, OH
03 June 2025

17417012R20022